Congressional
Research
Service

An Analysis of Charitable Giving and Donor Advised Funds

Molly F. Sherlock
Specialist in Public Finance

Jane G. Gravelle
Senior Specialist in Economic Policy

July 11, 2012

Congressional Research Service

7-5700

www.crs.gov

R42595

CRS Report for Congress
Prepared for Members and Committees of Congress

Summary

Congress has long been concerned with ensuring that contributions for which tax deductions are claimed directly benefit charitable activities. Private foundations, a traditional arrangement that allows donations to non-active charitable entities, typically pay grants out of earnings on donated assets. Another arrangement that is growing rapidly is the donor advised fund (DAF). A taxpayer contributes to a DAF, taking a tax deduction. The fund sponsor makes grants to active charities, advised by the donor. Unlike private foundations, DAFs are not required to pay out a certain proportion of assets as grants each year. DAFs have become increasingly popular in recent years, partly due to commercial funds (e.g., Fidelity) with limited traditional charitable interests.

Provisions enacted in the Pension Protection Act of 2006 (P.L. 109-280) required DAF sponsors to report data on grants. The data are reported at the sponsoring organization level, where sponsoring organizations may maintain multiple individual DAF accounts. The 2006 act also directed the Treasury Department to study DAFs, with Congress expressing particular interest in issues relating to potential restrictions on deductions and minimum payout requirements. The Treasury study was released in 2011. Senator Chuck Grassley, Senate Finance chairman at the time of the 2006 legislation, has criticized the study as being "disappointing and nonresponsive."

The Treasury did not recommend restrictions on deductions (such as those that apply to private foundations where grants are typically made out of earnings), appealing to the lack of legal control by the donor. However, evidence from public comments in the report and sponsor websites indicate that sponsoring organizations typically follow the donor's advice, thus suggesting that donors have effective control over donations and, in some cases, investments.

Private foundations have a 5% minimum payout rate (and actual payouts are only slightly above that amount). The Treasury also did not recommend a minimum payout for DAFs, indicating that more years of data are needed. The Treasury also appealed to the higher estimated average payout rate of DAF sponsoring organizations (9.3% in 2006) as compared to foundations.

This report uses 2008 data to examine the minimum payout requirement, finding results similar to those found by Treasury. The average payout rate was 13.1%. More than 181,000 individual DAF accounts were maintained by roughly 1,800 DAF sponsoring organizations. Most individual accounts were maintained by institutions with a large number of accounts (two-thirds of all DAF accounts were held by sponsoring organizations that maintained at least 500 accounts; nearly half of all DAF accounts were held by commercial DAF institutions). Assets in DAF accounts were $29.5 billion, contributions were $7.1 billion, and DAF accounts paid out $7.0 billion in grants.

Because DAF accounts have heterogeneous objectives, in some cases to manage giving with high payout rates and in others to establish an asset base, a DAF sponsor can have a high average payout rate although many accounts have little or no payout. In both 2006 and 2008, a substantial share of DAF sponsoring organizations paid out less than 5% of assets each year. To provide some insight into the payout behavior of individual DAF accounts, sponsoring organizations that reportedly maintained only one DAF account in 2008 are analyzed separately. Although the average payout rate was over 10%, more than 70% of DAF sponsoring organizations with a single DAF account paid out less than 5%, and 53% had no grants. In contrast, less than 4% of sponsors with 100 or more accounts, accounting for 87% of DAF accounts, have a payout rate of less than 5%. This suggests that a minimum payout rate for sponsors would not be effective; an effective minimum payout requirement would need to be applied to individual DAF accounts.

Contents

Figures

Tables

Appendixes

Contacts

A s Congress continues to examine various aspects of the tax code in the context of potential tax reform, the tax deduction for charitable contributions may come under scrutiny. Congress has long been concerned with ensuring that contributions for which tax deductions are claimed directly benefit charitable activities. Certain organizations that support charitable activities, however, may receive tax deductible charitable contributions today, but may not be required to use those funds for charitable purposes within any specific time frame. Thus, taxpayers may be claiming tax deductions for donated funds that are not immediately serving charitable purposes.

Certain types of organizations are given preferred tax status for supporting charitable activities, even if the organization is not directly involved in providing charitable goods or services. Private foundations, for example, make grants to charities but generally do not directly provide charitable goods and services. Grants are paid out of earnings on donated assets held by the foundation. Donor advised funds (DAFs) are another type of organization that serves to facilitate charitable giving, but are not directly involved in the provision of charitable goods and services. Like foundations, charitable contributions made directly to DAFs are tax deductible. Unlike foundations, DAFs are not subject to minimum payout requirements. DAFs have become increasingly popular in recent years, partly due to commercial fund sponsors (e.g., Fidelity and Vanguard) with limited traditional charitable interests.

Foundations, DAFs, and other organizations that invest contributed funds confer an additional tax benefit in the form of a tax exemption. This tax exemption allows organizations to accumulate assets without paying tax on earnings. During normal years (before the asset collapse during the recession) estimates suggested that the revenue loss from this tax benefit was even larger than that associated with charitable contributions deductions.[1] If charitable contributions were spent quickly, this benefit would be minimal. If contributions are held as assets and invested, the tax exemption may confer significant financial benefits.

Congress moved to impose greater restrictions on organizations that support, but are not directly involved in providing, charitable goods and services in the Pension Protection Act of 2006 (PPA; P.L. 109-280). Notably, certain types of supporting organizations were subject to a minimum payout ratio of 5% of assets under provisions enacted as part of the PPA. DAFs, however, were not subject to payout requirements. The PPA did impose additional reporting requirements on DAFs, and requested a Treasury Department study of DAFs along with supporting organizations.

The Treasury Department's study was released in 2011.[2] The Treasury Report was criticized by Senator Chuck Grassley, chairman of the Senate Finance Committee in 2006, as being "disappointing and nonresponsive."[3] This report reviews the findings of the Treasury study with respect to DAFs and provides additional analysis of payout behavior of DAFs (one of Congress's primary concerns when requesting the study) using data from the 2008 Internal Revenue Service (IRS) Statistics of Income (SOI) public use file for tax-exempt organizations.

---

[1] See CRS Report RL34608, *Tax Issues Relating to Charitable Contributions and Organizations*, by Jane G. Gravelle and Molly F. Sherlock.

[2] U.S. Department of the Treasury, *Report to Congress on Supporting Organizations and Donor Advised Funds* December 2011, http://www.treasury.gov/resource-center/tax-policy/documents/supporting-organizations-and-donor-advised-funds-12-5-11.pdf. Referenced as "Treasury Report" below.

[3] See "Grassley: Treasury Misses the Mark on Chance to Shut Down Charitable Loopholes" http://www.grassley.senate.gov/news/Article.cfm?customel_dataPageID_1502=38154.

Recent Developments in the Tax Treatment of Donor Advised Funds (DAFs)

Donor advised funds allow individuals to make a gift to a fund in a sponsoring organization. Sponsoring organizations are charities that are allowed to receive tax-deductible donations. The gift is irrevocable, as in the case of a gift to a foundation or any other charity. The donor does not legally oversee the payment of grants to charities from the fund, which is determined by the sponsoring organizations. Donors make recommendations for grants (hence donor advised), and there is general agreement that these recommendations determine, with few exceptions, the contributions. For example, the Treasury Report indicated that all respondents providing public comments reported no conflicts with their donor's advice and agreed that the donor's recommendations are generally followed.[4]

DAFs first appeared in the 1930s, largely sponsored by community foundations and involving relatively large contributions. Over time, these DAFs continued to be largely sponsored by community foundations, and, to a lesser extent, religious organizations. However, in the early 1990s, investment firms began to set up charitable organizations to sponsor DAFs. Fidelity established a DAF sponsoring organization in 1992, and other financial institutions quickly followed.[5]

Currently, numerous commercial DAF sponsors operate, with Fidelity, Schwab, and Vanguard being the largest in terms of asset size. The rapid growth in DAFs is associated with the appearance of commercial DAF sponsors which now control roughly one-third of DAF assets. Community foundations account for 43% of DAF assets and religious organizations 15%.[6] Commercial DAFs tend to allow relatively small contributions and do not have a direct charitable interest, as is the case for the other DAF sponsors, such as community foundations, religious organizations, education, health, or other charitable organizations.

DAFs may be used to hold funds temporarily, which may be useful for year end planning, and distributions out of the contributions may be made quickly.[7] They also may be used in the same way as private foundations: with a large contribution to the fund, which is then used to generate income and make grants largely out of income. In cases where DAFs' advisor status can be inherited, such funds can exist in perpetuity, just as most foundations do.

Not only can this treatment, compared to ordinary charitable giving, confer additional tax benefits by allowing fund earnings to accumulate tax free, it can facilitate the contributions of appreciated

---

[4] See Treasury Report p. 69: "No respondent reported ongoing disagreements with donors over the appropriateness of potential grants, and all respondents said that, in general, donor advice was followed."

[5] For a discussion of the differences between the early DAFs and the more recent commercial DAFs, see Ellie Winninghoff, *Impact Investing Through DAFs*, November 2, 2011, http://www.fa-mag.com/green/news/9044-impact-investing-through-dafs.html.

[6] See Treasury Report, p. 48. These figures are based on 2006 data. Other national DAF sponsors and education sponsored DAFs accounted for most of the remainder (5% and 4% respectively). Treasury also reviews the growth in DAFs in recent years.

[7] A recent news article discussed the use of DAF accounts to accelerate contributions, given the possibility of restrictions on charitable contributions in dealing with the budget deficit. See "Invasion of the Charity Snatchers!" *Wall Street Journal*, June 8, 2012, http://online.wsj.com/article/SB10001424052702303296604577450451929765874.html?mod=ITP_businessandfinance_4. A version appeared in the print edition on July 9, p. B7.

property. A DAF can permit the contribution of a large indivisible appreciated property such as real estate. When property is not divisible, the contribution cannot be spread across many charitable donors or donated over time. Contributions of property can be made to a DAF, sold without tax consequences, and the proceeds used to make smaller subsequent contributions to multiple recipients or donations over time. Donors receive another tax benefit when they donate appreciated property, because they do not have to pay capital gains tax on the appreciation, while at the same time deducting the charitable gift at market value in most cases.

DAFs Versus Foundations

As shown in **Table 1**, DAFs, as ordinary charities, have more generous treatment than private foundations in several respects.[8] Only publicly traded property such as corporate stock is eligible for a deduction for the full fair market value when donated to a private foundation. Property such as real estate is allowed a deduction for fair market value when contributed to a public charity including a DAF, but is limited to cost basis when contributed to a private foundation. The limits on the share of income that can be donated in any one year to charities, which contributions to DAFs fall under (50% for cash contributions and 30% for gifts of appreciated property) are more generous than for contributions to foundations (30% for cash and 20% for gifts of appreciated property). There are no minimum payout requirements (which could require a certain percentage of assets be paid out in grants each year) or excise taxes. Prior to the 2006 act, DAFs had the same rules on self dealing as public charities, although they are now subject to many private foundation rules (such as disallowing transactions with the donor, such as loans). DAFs may also have some advantages outside of tax benefits. The cost of setting up and administering a DAF is smaller than in the case of a foundation, which can be important for smaller contributions. Where privacy in making contributions is desired, DAFs can be superior since individual DAF grants are not public.

Private foundations have more favorable treatment than DAFs in two respects. Donors who establish foundations (or their heirs) may continue to control the foundation by being a director or trustee and can receive a salary for services, while donors to DAFs do not have legal control over investment or grant choices. Wealthy individuals, for example, may leave large shares of their estate to a foundation, and their children may be involved in its operation, conferring social status as well as possible employment. Evidence suggests, however, that donors to DAFs have effective control over grants, and to some extent investments, because sponsoring organizations typically follow the donor's advice. The second benefit for foundations is greater freedom in grant making: they can make grants to individuals and to non-profit organizations for charitable purposes, if certain requirements are met.

---

[8] See also Ruth Masterson, *The Best of Both Worlds: Using Private Foundations and Donor Advised Funds: A Guide for Professional Advisors*, Association of Small Foundations, http://www.fidelitycharitable.org/docs/Using-Private-Foundations-and-Donor-Advised-Funds.pdf. For a brief guide to these difference, see National Philanthropic Trust, *Donor-Advised Funds vs. Private Foundations*, http://www.nptrust.org/donor-advised-funds/daf_vs_foundation/.

Table 1. Comparison of Features of DAFs and Private Foundations

	DAFs	Foundations
Features Beneficial to DAFs		
Deduction for Gifts of Appreciated Property	Fair Market Value	Fair Market Value for Pub icly Traded Stocks; Cost Basis Otherwise
Income Limits for Cash Gifts	50%	30%
Income Limits for Property Gifts	30%	20%
Minimum Pay Out Requirements	None	5%
Excise Taxes	None	1-2% of Investment Income
Start Up Costs	None	Typically Substantial Legal and Other Fees
Start Up Time	Immediate	Can Take Weeks or Months
Administrative Costs	Usually Less than 0.85% plus Investment Management Fees	2.5% to 4% of Assets
Privacy	Donor's Name Can be Confidential	Public Filings Report Grants, Trustees, etc.
Features Beneficial To Foundations		
Control	Donors Advise on Grants, and In Some Cases Investments, but have No Legal Control	Donors and Designates Can Control Investments and Grants, Receive Salary
Freedom in Grant Making	Limited to Charitable Organizations	Can Make Grants to Individuals and Non-Profits Under Certain Circumstances

Source: Data on the administrative costs and information on start up times are from National Philanthropic Trust, Donor-Advised Funds vs. Private Foundations, http://www.nptrust.org/donor-advised-funds/ daf_vs_foundation.

These parallels to foundations, along with the rapid growth of DAFs including commercial DAFs, coupled with some reports of abuse, caused much of the legislative attention to DAFs (as well as supporting organizations) leading up to the 2006 legislation. Following some initial studies by staff of the Senate Finance Committee, hearings were held in 2005 that addressed DAFs as well as supporting organizations, gifts of appreciated property, and other charitable issues.[9] In 2006, a GAO study recommended additional reporting of information on DAFs.[10]

The Pension Protection Act of 2006 (P.L. 109-280) made two changes with respect to DAFs: it required reporting of the aggregate assets, grants, and contributions for sponsoring organizations

---

[9] See hearing on Charities and Charitable Giving: Proposals for Reform, Senate Finance Committee, April 2005, http://finance.senate.gov/hearings/hearing/?id=489a7e96-d336-be14-8262-f27b2f90024e See particularly testimony by Mark Everson, Commissioner of Internal Revenue, http://finance.senate.gov/imo/media/doc/metest040505.pdf and of Jane G. Gravelle, Congressional Research Service, http://finance.senate.gov/imo/media/doc/jgtest040505.pdf for discussions on donor-advised funds.

[10] Tax Exempt Organizations: Collecting More Data on Donor-Advised Funds and Supporting Organizations Could Help Address Compliance Challenges, GAO-06-799, July 2006, http://www.gao.gov/new.items/d06799.pdf.

and provided for penalty taxes and restrictions on grants that did not meet required standards or that benefited the donor or the donor's family. It did not impose minimum payout requirements on DAFs (only on certain supporting organizations) and did not alter the income limits for contributions. Rather, it mandated a study of these issues by Treasury.

Questions Addressed in the 2011 Treasury Report

In mandating the study of DAFs and supporting organizations, Congress specifically asked four questions of the Treasury Department:

1. Are existing charitable deductions (which have more generous limits and deduction amounts than those for private foundations) appropriate considering the use of contributions (type, extent, and timing) or the use for the benefit of the donor?

2. Should DAFs be subject to a payout ratio?

3. Is an advisory role in the investment or distribution of donated funds consistent with a completed gift?[11]

4. Do these issues apply to other charitable gifts?

The remaining sections examine the first three questions as they relate to DAFs, how Treasury answered them, and what further policy options might be considered.

Should DAF Contribution Rules Be More Restrictive?

The 2011 Treasury Report made comments regarding restrictions on giving as a percentage of income and on the treatment of gifts of appreciated property. As noted above, individuals can contribute up to half of their income in cash contributions to charities but only 30% to private foundations. For gifts of appreciated property, 30% of income can be donated to charities but only 20% to private foundations. For gifts of appreciated property, deductions for fair market value cannot be taken for other than publicly traded assets in the case of gifts to foundations.

Treasury took the position that these rules should not be changed based on the legal right of DAF sponsors to make grants and investment allocations, and the inability of the donor to control the sponsoring organization, which they contrasted with the right of the donor to a private foundation to retain control of the foundation. As stated in the Treasury Report: "Because donors to DAFs ... are like donors to other public charities, giving up both control of the contributed assets and the ability to control the donee organization, the deduction rules seem appropriate."[12]

This position can be questioned. First, it is the DAF account, not the sponsoring organization, in which the donor presumably has an interest. Donors would not reasonably expect to control Fidelity Charity, which has more than 50,000 individual DAF accounts. The question is how much actual control donors have over their individual account. This individual account is

---

[11] Currently a charitable donation is not complete if the donor maintains control over the gift, its sale, or further use.

[12] Treasury Report, p. 80.

frequently referred to in discussions, including in the Treasury Report, as a substitute for setting up a private foundation.

With respect to recommending grants there is fairly compelling evidence that although donors legally only recommend grants, in practice they determine when and how the funds are distributed because sponsoring organizations typically follow their advice. In the public comments summarized in the Treasury Report,

> No respondent reported ongoing disagreements with donors over the appropriateness of potential grants, and all respondents said that, in general, donor advice was followed. However, one respondent was critical of the relationship between the donor and the sponsoring organization of the DAF. The respondent expressed concern that many such arrangements 'appear to give DAF donors de facto control over investment and distribution decisions.'[13]

A review of relevant websites supports this notion. Consider an example from the Alaska Community Foundation, in answer to the question, "Are Grant Requests Ever Denied?":

> Sometimes. We have a legal obligation not to approve grants that don't meet criteria established by law. This includes a grant request that is not charitable in nature, provides a direct benefit to the donor advisor or a related party, or is directed to an individual. We will always work closely with you to find alternatives that help you meet your grant-making goals.[14]

As to the question of whether grants have to be made every year, the Alaska Community Foundation website states the following:

> No. Grants do not have to be made every year. However, if no grants have been made from a fund for two years, we will attempt to contact the fund advisors. After several years of inactivity and if we are unable to contact you, a fund may be turned into a designated, unrestricted or field of interest fund as near as possible to your original intent.

In other words, this sponsoring organization advertises that it will typically follow the donors' requests and work closely with the donor to find alternatives if the request has to be denied, and that the sponsoring organization will generally not make other grants from the donor-advisors' account unless there are years of inactivity and an inability to contact the advisor.

This website is not atypical. For example, the largest commercial DAF organization, Fidelity, states the following:

> Fidelity Charitable only approves grants that are used exclusively in furtherance of charitable purposes. In accordance with that policy, Fidelity Charitable reserves the right to perform additional due diligence and to decline to make a recommended grant to a charitable organization, including, without limitation, (i) where the grant will confer a more than incidental benefit on an Account Holder, other person with grant recommendation privileges, or other third party; (ii) where the grant will be used for lobbying, for political contributions, or to support political campaign activities; (iii) where the grant will be used for improper purposes; (iv) where the Account Holder and related persons control the organization; (v)

---

[13] Treasury Report, p. 69.

[14] See http://www.alaskacf.org/givingopportunities/typesoffunds/donoradvisedfunds/tabid/205/default.aspx.

where Fidelity Charitable provides a substantial portion of the organization's public support; and (vi) for other reasons in accordance with Fidelity Charitable policies. Remedial actions may include but are not limited to requiring that the grant be returned or that the Account Holder make an additional nondeductible contribution.[15]

Fidelity does have a policy of an overall distribution for the organization (not each account) of at least 5%. Were Fidelity to need to make additional grants, Fidelity indicates they would request grants be made from the accounts with no payouts. However, Fidelity would still consult with the account holder for recommendations. Apparently, this need is never necessary in any case as they typically make grants of 20% of net assets.[16]

Investment policies appear to be more variable, although in many cases the donors are probably less interested in the investment allocations than in the recipients of grants. Fidelity offers donors choices of investment allocations out of their basic funds, and for large donations, the ability to recommend a financial advisor. The Alaskan foundation mentioned earlier manages the funds without direction from the donor. The American Endowment Foundation and The Renaissance Charitable Gift Fund allow investment control of each account.[17]

Essentially in each of the other issues the Treasury addressed for this question, including whether there should be restrictions on the donation of appreciated property and on the timing of deductions (allow deductions without ensuring that the money will be spent in a reasonable period for a charitable purpose) the Treasury Report reverts to this same argument: that contributions to DAFs are no different from contributions to other charities (as opposed to private foundations) because the donor does not retain legal control over the donation.

Another point that appears in public comments is that commercial DAFs, in particular, may have no incentive to pay out funds or encourage donors to do so. The public comments noted one respondent as pointing to "an inherent tension between the incentives of NDAF financial advisors and charitable purposes."[18] (NDAFs refer to national DAF sponsors and are primarily composed of commercial DAFs.) Even Fidelity's stated commitment to at least a 5% payout rate is apparently a non-binding constraint because a sufficient portion of their accounts are held by donors who make significant donations.

As Congress evaluates the position of the Treasury Department on whether DAFs should be treated as private foundations or as public charities, an important issue is whether, for policy-making purposes, the restricted legal rights of the donors or the de facto practices should rule. It is relatively clear from the evidence, including in the Treasury Report, that the donor-advisors effectively determine the grants made from DAFs and in some cases also have control over how investments are made. In these respects, they may be more similar to contributions to foundations

---

[15] See http://www.fidelitycharitable.org/docs/Gift-Fund-Policy-Guidelines.pdf.

[16] Ibid, "Historically, Fidelity Charitable has made grants of more than 20% of average net total assets to charities each year. The formal grant making policy requires that minimum annual grants, on an overall basis, be greater than 5% of average net assets on a fiscal five-year rolling basis. If this requirement is not met in a fiscal year, Fidelity Charitable will ask for grant recommendations from Giving Accounts that have not had grant activity of at least 5% of the Giving Account's average net assets over the same five-year period. If Account Holders on these Giving Accounts do not make grant recommendations within 60 days, Fidelity Charitable will transfer the required amounts to the Trustees' Philanthropy Fund (described on page 28), from which the Trustees will make grants at their sole discretion."

[17] http://www.aefonline.org/investments.htm; http://www.rcgf.org/docs/DAF-Circular.pdf.

[18] Treasury Report, p. 68.

than to contributions to public charities. Contributions to private foundations are subject to greater restrictions on the share of income that can be donated, more reporting requirements and restrictions, and minimum distributions.

Should DAFs Be Subject to a Minimum Distribution Requirement?

The Treasury Report's information related to this issue included solicitation of comments and an analysis of the data on DAFs reported on IRS Form 990 informational returns of tax-exempt organizations for 2006.

Comments, primarily from community foundations and national DAFs (NDAFs), opposed payout ratios on the grounds that aggregate distributions exceed the payout ratio for private foundations. Some comments described rules and restrictions being voluntarily applied by certain sponsoring organizations that addressed payout requirements. For example, comments noted that organizations may choose to force grants if no grants are made over several years. In general, some thought a 5% minimum distribution requirement was acceptable if applied to the overall sponsoring organization and not to each individual DAF account. They also argued that monitoring accounts would be costly and that donors may take a 5% rate as a guideline. Some respondents, however, expressed the view that the accumulation of assets for undefined charitable purposes supported minimum payouts for individual DAF accounts.

Using the 990 data, the Treasury Report examined the size distribution, allocation across types, and payout ratios. They found some over-reporting of payout rates in the 990 sample. The overall average payout rate across all DAF sponsors was 9.3%. However, the payout rates varied substantially. Arranged by payout rate, at the 25th percentile, the payout rate was zero, meaning that at least 25% of sponsoring organizations did not pay out grants. At the median, the payout rate was 0.6%, while it was 10.5% at the 75th percentile. DAF accounts and assets are heavily concentrated in the larger DAF sponsors and, with multiple accounts, one is unlikely to observe zero payout rates among these groups. Because of the greater concentration of assets in larger DAF sponsors, the dollar weighted payout rate is higher, 15.4%.

The Treasury Report generally concludes that it would be premature to make a recommendation regarding a minimum payout based on 2006 data (2006 was the first year that DAF data was reported on the Form 990 informational return). In discussing this issue, the report notes that the aggregate payout rate of 9.3% (across organizations) is higher than that of foundations, which hover slightly above the required payout of 5%. This payout ratio is an average of payout ratios across the organizations; the dollar weighted payout ratio is 15.4%, indicating that sponsoring organizations with larger amounts of assets have higher payout rates. The Treasury Report notes that payout ratios are only available for the sponsoring organization and not for the individual DAF account.

The higher pay-out rate for DAFs, as compared to foundations, could be interpreted as indicating no need for a minimum payout. However, there is reason to question this interpretation. Private foundations are typically established to exist in perpetuity and to make grants out of their earnings. DAF contributors are more heterogeneous. Funds may be set up as an endowment type, similar to private foundations, or for annual giving where most funds are paid out. For example, Schwab Charitable, in listing advantages of a DAF, begins with separating year-end tax planning from charitable giving decisions, followed by simplifying tax preparation by having only one charitable deduction, and benefits associated with an account used for charitable contribution management and tax planning.[19] The co-existence of these types of accounts within one DAF sponsor mean that a high payout rate, by comparison with foundation standards, could conceal a significant share of accounts with a payout rate of less than 5%. For example, if 20% of accounts paid out an average of 80%, then 80% of accounts could have no payouts but the payout ratio overall would be 16%.

This report analyzes the 2008 DAF sample, examining not only the payout rates of the sponsoring organizations, but also the rates for those organizations with only one DAF account, which might provide some insight into the characteristics of individual DAF accounts that cannot be observed. As shown below, over 70% of DAF accounts in these organizations paid less than 5% in grants, and 54% made no payments at all.

Completed Gifts

The third question asked of the Treasury was whether a contribution to a DAF should be considered a completed gift. Completed gifts require that the donor no longer have control over donations. Treasury considered these contributions completed gifts based on legal ownership and control. This question is basically a legal question, rather than one reflecting policy choices. Nevertheless, some of the received comments questioned whether certain types of gifts were in fact completed gifts. Questions were raised with respect to gifts of appreciated property to donor advised funds that involved first rights of refusal on sale to the donor, calls (charity must offer to sell to the donor at a set price), or puts (donor must purchase from the charity at a set price).

Analysis of 2008 Donor Advised Fund Data

The analysis presented below uses data from the 2008 Internal Revenue Service (IRS) Statistics of Income (SOI) Form 990 public use file (see **Appendix A** for more information). This dataset contains information as reported by a sample of tax-exempt organizations on the Form 990, which is an informational return. The 2008 return asks organizations to provide information on donor advised funds, including the number of funds maintained, contributions to and grants from DAFs, and the total value of DAF assets.[20]

Since 2005, the IRS has been gathering information on DAFs on the Form 990 informational returns filed by tax-exempt entities. Prior to 2005, the primary resource for information on DAFs was an annual survey of DAF sponsoring organizations conducted by the *Chronicle of Philanthropy*. The data reported on the IRS Form 990 is an improvement over the survey-generated data that was previously available. Nonetheless, the Form 990 data has limitations.

One of the primary limitations of the IRS Form 990 data is its aggregate nature. Data on DAFs is reported at the sponsoring organization level, and not at the individual DAF account level. Thus,

---

[19] Posted at http://www.schwabcharitable.org/public/charitable/how_the_program_works/key_advantages.

[20] Beginning in 2008, this information can be found in Schedule D of the Form 990. Similar information was also requested on 2006 and 2007 forms. However, the Form 990 was redesigned in 2008, at which point the information was requested on Schedule D.

for organizations that sponsor more than one DAF, information on contributions, grants, and payout rates per individual DAF are not available.

The 2011 Treasury Report was the first comprehensive report on sponsoring organizations and DAFs that used data as reported on the IRS Form 990. The Treasury Report used data from the 2006 Form 990 informational returns. The analysis below uses information as reported on 2008 Form 990s. In a number of instances, the results presented below are compared to the results as reported in the 2011 Treasury Report.

Comparisons between the Treasury Report and the analysis below should be viewed with caution for a number of reasons. First, the IRS Form 990 was redesigned in both 2006 and 2008. Given that these forms were unfamiliar to filers, there is greater risk that the reported information may contain errors. Second, while on the 2008 Form 990 DAF-related information is reported in a separate section, this was not the case in 2006. Finally, the analysis here is based on a sample of returns as reported in the public use file. Thus, all reported statistics are estimated population totals based on this sample. The more observations with reporting errors, particularly those with high sampling weights, the less accurate the population estimates.

Number of Accounts at DAF Sponsoring Organizations

Analysis of the IRS SOI data indicates that, in 2008, more than 181,000 individual DAF fund accounts were maintained (see **Table 2**). In 2008, there were roughly 1,818 organizations maintaining at least one DAF account.[21] Most charitable organizations that sponsor DAFs maintain very few accounts. Roughly one-third of all organizations claiming to have DAFs reported that only one fund was maintained.[22] Roughly half of all DAF sponsoring organizations reported that five or less DAF funds were held. On average, DAF sponsoring organizations had 100 accounts.[23]

A small percentage of DAF sponsoring organizations held a large number of DAF accounts. Fifty-one organizations (or roughly 3% of all DAF sponsoring organizations) reported having 500 or more individual DAF accounts (see **Table 2**). More than 121,000 of all DAF accounts (or two-thirds of all DAF accounts) are maintained by institutions that have 500 or more individual accounts. The fact that a large proportion of individual DAF accounts are maintained by a small number of DAF sponsoring organizations explains why the number of DAF accounts per organization is highly skewed.

---

[21] Several other organizations either indicated that they maintained DAFs, or reported a positive value for aggregate DAF assets.

[22] This number could be overstated if organizations filing the Form 990 reported only one DAF and aggregate contributions, grants, and DAF values, which may have been spread across multiple DAF accounts.

[23] This average is for DAF sponsoring organizations that reported maintaining at least one DAF.

**Table 2. Number of Individual DAF Accounts Held
by DAF Sponsoring Organizations**

2008

Number of DAFs Maintained	Number of Sponsoring Organizations	Share of DAF Sponsoring Organizations	Number of Individual DAF Accounts	Share of Individual DAF Accounts
1	626	34.4%	626	0.3%
2 – 19	566	31.1%	3,289	1.8%
20 – 99	403	22.2%	18,535	10.2%
100 – 499	171	9.4%	37,915	20.9%
500+	51	2.8%	121,064	66.7%
Totals	**1,818**	**100%**	**181,429**	**100%**

Source: CRS analysis of 2008 IRS SOI Form 990 data.

Notes: This information is based on a sample of sponsoring organizations, weighted to reflect the population. Columns may not sum due to rounding. The number of organizations sponsoring DAFs and the number of individual DAF accounts are estimated population totals based on the 2008 IRS SOI Form 990 sample. See the appendixes for more information.

The 2011 Treasury Report on DAFs reported similar statistics. Using 2006 data, the Treasury Report estimated that more than 160,000 individual DAF accounts were maintained by 2,398 tax-exempt organizations. On average, DAF sponsoring organizations maintained 85 accounts in 2006, while the median organization maintained 4 accounts.[24]

Data on contributions, grants paid, and DAF asset values are only available at the DAF sponsoring-organization level. Since most DAF accounts are held by organizations maintaining multiple DAF accounts, little is known about the characteristics of the majority of individual DAF accounts.

DAF Assets

In 2008, DAF sponsoring organizations reported a total of $29.5 billion in DAF assets on their Form 990s. On average, assets per DAF account in 2008 were roughly $162,000 (see **Table 3**).[25] Sponsoring organizations maintaining a larger number of DAFs tended to have fewer assets per DAF account than organizations that reported only one or fewer than 20 DAF accounts. The majority of DAF assets are held by organizations that sponsor a large number of DAFs—87% of all DAF assets are held by sponsoring organizations that maintain 100 or more individual DAF accounts.

---

[24] Treasury Report, pp. 45-46 and p. 56.

[25] This figure is equal to the total DAF assets in 2008 divided by the total number of DAF accounts reportedly maintained in 2008. The Treasury 2011 study on DAFs, using 2006 data, reported a distribution of average assets per DAF account. In the Treasury 2011 study, average assets per account were calculated for each sponsoring organization individually. Average assets per DAF was reported as the mean of each organization's average assets per account. Using this methodology, average assets per DAF are $369,455. For additional information on the distribution of average assets per DAF across sponsoring organizations, see **Appendix B**.

There is substantial variation in average assets per DAF account across sponsoring organizations. A few large organizations have high average assets per DAF, causing these averages to be skewed upwards. At the DAF sponsoring organization level, the median sponsoring organization has an average asset value per DAF of $55,178 (see **Appendix B** for more information on the distribution of the average asset value per DAF across DAF sponsoring organizations).

Table 3. Average Assets per DAF Account

2008

Number of DAFs Maintained	Average Assets per DAF Account	Share of Total DAF Assets
1	$646,795	1.4%
2 – 19	$207,211	2.3%
20 – 99	$153,791	9.7%
100 – 499	$186,503	24.0%
500+	$152,323	62.6%
Total	$162,360	100%

Source: CRS analysis of 2008 IRS SOI Form 990 data.

Notes: This information is based on a sample of sponsoring organizations, weighted to reflect the population. Average assets per DAF account for each group are the sum of total DAF assets within that group, divided by the number of individual DAF accounts, within that group. Columns may not sum due to rounding. The number of organizations sponsoring DAFs and the number of individual DAF accounts are estimated population totals based on the 2008 IRS SOI Form 990 sample. See the appendixes for more information.

The 2011 Treasury Report on DAFs reported that in 2006, DAF assets were $31.1 billion. The National Philanthropic Trust's 2011 report indicated DAF assets of $30.2 billion in 2008.[26] The National Philanthropic Trust's 2010 and 2011 reports show that DAF assets declined as a result of the recession that began in December 2007.[27] However, when looking only at data from the National Philanthropic Trust, DAF assets in 2008 appear higher than what was reported in 2006. This difference may reflect possible reporting errors in the data or different samples, and underscores the importance of using caution when comparing DAF data as collected from different sources.

Contributions To and Grants From DAF Accounts

In 2008, total contributions to DAF accounts were reported to be $7.1 billion. Total charitable giving by individuals in 2008 was roughly $214 billion.[28] Thus, contributions to DAFs represented roughly 3.3% of total individual charitable giving in 2008. On average, DAF

---

[26] National Philanthropic Trust, 2011 Donor-Advised Fund Report, http://www.nptrust.org/images/uploads/ 2011%20Donor-Advised-Fund-Report(1).pdf.

[27] 2010 Report at http://www.nptrust.org/images/uploads/DAF-Report-2010.pdf.

[28] Giving USA. Giving USA figures were used here rather than contributions reported on the Form 990 since Form 990 data excludes contributions made to small organizations and organizations exempt from filing informational returns.

sponsoring organizations received $3.9 million in contributions in 2008.[29] The average contribution per DAF account, in 2008, was roughly $39,103.[30]

The average contribution per DAF account is substantially higher for sponsoring organizations that reportedly maintain only one DAF account (see **Table 4**). This figure is driven by the fact that a few organizations received very large contributions. Approximately one-third of DAF sponsoring organizations reportedly maintaining only one DAF reported having received positive contributions in 2008. Among the organizations reporting positive contributions, the average contribution was $1.3 million. Thus, there is substantial variation in contribution levels to individual DAF accounts for sponsoring organizations with only one DAF. This variation is likely masked by the aggregate nature of the data for organizations maintaining more than one DAF. It is also possible that some organizations that report maintaining only one DAF account have misreported this information, stating that only one DAF is sponsored when the organization actually maintains multiple accounts.[31]

The 2011 Treasury Report on DAFs found that, in 2006, total contributions to DAFs was $9.0 billion. The lower contributions reported in 2008 could reflect reduced giving during the recession or reporting errors in the Form 990 data.[32] The National Philanthropic Trust's 2011 DAF study notes that contributions to DAFs declined from 2007 through 2009, before increasing again in 2010.[33] However, the National Philanthropic Trust's 2010 report found that total contributions in 2008 were higher than those in 2006.[34] Total charitable giving also declined between 2007 through 2009, before increasing again in 2010.[35]

In 2008, DAF sponsoring organizations reported paying out $7.0 billion in grants to charitable organizations. On average, $38,641 in grants were paid per DAF account (see **Table 4**). As was the case with contributions, DAF sponsoring organizations that reportedly maintained only one DAF paid out average grants per DAF that were substantially higher than the average grant per DAF paid out by organizations maintaining more than one DAF. As was noted above, this statistic might be the result of DAF sponsoring organizations reporting the maintenance of a single DAF account, when the organization actually maintains multiple accounts.

---

[29] The median value was $29,898, suggesting that the typical organization sponsoring DAFs receives less in contributions than is received on average. If organizations reporting that they received no contributions are excluded, the median value is $308,102 and the average value $6.0 million. The sample suggests more than 650 DAF sponsoring organizations reportedly received no contributions to DAFs in 2008.

[30] This average is calculated at the total value of DAF contributions divided by the total number of individual DAF accounts maintained.

[31] Inspections of 2007 and 2009 Form 990s for some of the largest organizations reporting very large contributions to a single DAF account did not turn up any immediately transparent errors.

[32] There may also be reporting errors in the data. Thus, comparisons in contributions across years should be made with caution.

[33] National Philanthropic Trust, 2011 Donor-Advised Fund Report, http://www.nptrust.org/images/uploads/2011%20Donor-Advised-Fund-Report(1).pdf.

[34] National Philanthropic Trust, 2010 Donor-Advised Fund Report, http://www.nptrust.org/images/uploads/DAF-Report-2010.pdf.

[35] Giving USA Foundation, *Giving USA 2011 The Annual Report on Philanthropy for the Year 2010*, 2011, p. 53.

Table 4. Average Contributions and Grants per DAF Account

2008

Number of DAFs Maintained	Average Contribution per DAF Account	Average Grant Paid per DAF Account
I	$430,178[a]	$409,489[b]
2 – 19	$48,233	$46,858
20 – 99	$37,984	$29,643
100 – 499	$40.290	$39,334
500+	$36,662	$37,660
All	$39,103	$38,641

Source: CRS analysis of 2008 IRS SOI Form 990 data.

Notes: This information is based on a sample of sponsoring organizations, weighted to reflect the population. Average contributions and average grants for each group are calculated as total contributions (grants) reported by sponsoring organizations within the group divided by total DAFs maintained by sponsoring organizations within the group. For DAF sponsoring organizations with only one reported DAF account, it is possible that there are reporting errors in the data, with DAF sponsoring organizations reporting only one account when multiple accounts were maintained.

a. There are a number of organizations that reportedly maintained only one DAF account reportedly received very large (multi-million dollar) contributions. These few organizations drove this average up. Further, roughly two-thirds of all DAF sponsoring organizations reporting only to have maintained one DAF also reported zero contributions during 2008. Thus, the average contribution received by those that received positive contributions and only sponsored one DAF account was substantially higher, at $1.3 million.

b. An estimated 292 DAF sponsoring organizations that maintained only one DAF account paid out grants. Among those that did pay out grants, the average grant paid was $876,984.

DAFs that Do Not Pay Out Grants

A number of DAF sponsoring organizations did not pay out any grants during 2008. Out of the 1,828 DAF sponsoring organizations included in the sample, an estimated 453 did not pay out any grants.[36] The organizations that sponsored DAFs but did not pay grants held a total of $280.4 million in assets in 2008. It is not known how much in additional DAF assets is held in individual accounts that do not pay grants, since grant data are reported on aggregate at the sponsoring organization level.

Most of the DAF sponsoring organizations that did not pay out any grants sponsored only one or very few DAFs (334 of the 453 DAF sponsoring organizations that did not report paying out any grants maintained a single DAF account).[37] Since grants paid are only reported in aggregate, at the DAF sponsoring organization level, information on individual DAFs that do not pay out each year is not available. It is likely that there are many individual DAF accounts maintained by sponsoring organizations with multiple accounts that did not pay out any grants in 2008. Roughly

---

[36] The 1,828 DAF sponsoring organizations were represented by 541 observations in the IRS SOI sample. Of the 541 observations sampled, 83 did not report making any grants in 2008. Based on the sampling weights given in the IRS SOI file, these 83 observations represent 453 DAF sponsoring organizations. All of these organizations reported positive DAF assets.

[37] Forty-seven sample observations reported to have maintained a single DAF account and not to have paid out any grants in 2008. Using the given sampling weights, these organizations represented 334 DAF sponsoring organizations.

half of the DAF sponsoring organizations that reportedly maintained only one DAF account did not pay out any grants in 2008.[38]

DAF Payout Rate

Since data on DAFs are reported at the sponsoring organization level, data on individual account payouts are not available. Nonetheless, evaluating payout rates at the sponsoring organization level may provide some insight into the proportion of funds that are being distributed for charitable purposes.

The payout rates for DAF sponsoring organizations calculated here are not directly comparable to the payout rates for private foundations. For private foundations, certain taxes and administrative expenses can be counted toward meeting the five percent payout requirement.

DAF sponsoring organizations paid out $7.0 billion in grants from DAF accounts in 2008. Total DAF assets were $29.5 billion at the end of 2008. Approximately 19.2% of total assets available for distribution were paid out, where total assets available for distribution is the sum of end-of-year assets and grants paid from DAFs.[39] Using 2006 data, the Treasury Report found that 15.4% of assets available for distribution were paid out.[40]

Aggregate DAF payout rates at the sponsoring organization level were constructed to examine sponsoring organization payout behavior. For each organization, the payout rate was calculated as total grants paid from DAFs divided by total assets available for grant-making (or end-of-year DAF assets plus grants paid from DAFs during the year).[41] An average payout rate can then be calculated as the arithmetic mean of the individual DAF sponsoring organizations' payout rates.

In 2008, the average payout rate across DAF sponsoring organizations was 13.1%. However, there was substantial variation in payout rates across sponsoring organizations (see **Figure 1**). The median payout rate was 6.1%, and the average is skewed by the payout rates of organizations with unusually large payouts. In 2008, 43% of DAF sponsoring organizations had an average payout of less than 5%; 26% did not report a payout.[42] The payout at the 25th percentile was 0.0% in 2008, while the payout at the 75th percentile was 19.5% (see **Table B-1**).

---

[38] In total, there were 626 DAF sponsoring organizations in 2008 that reportedly maintained only one DAF account (see **Table 1**). There were 334 DAF sponsoring organizations that reportedly maintained only one account that reported zero grants paid out in 2008.

[39] This follows the definition provided in the 2011 Treasury Report. The Treasury Report notes that total assets available for grant-making is the sum of DAF assets at the start of the year, contributions to DAFs during the year, and investment income earned by DAFs. This sum is equal to the sum of the year-end value of DAF assets and grants made from DAFs during the year.

[40] Treasury Report, p. 49.

[41] In computing this payout rate, only DAF sponsoring organizations that reported maintaining at least one DAF and organizations that reported positive asset values for 2008 were included. The population of DAF sponsoring organizations of 1,738 is represented by a sample of 530 observations.

[42] A total of 774 organizations represented by a sample of 156 observations reported a payout rate of less than 5%.

Figure 1. Distribution of Payout Rate Across DAF Sponsoring Organizations
2008

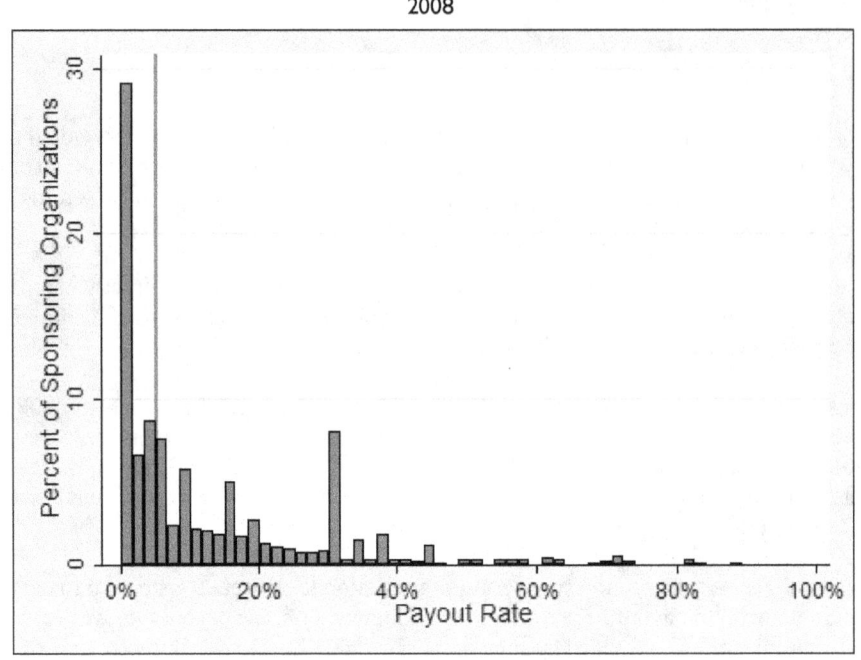

Source: CRS analysis of 2008 IRS SOI Form 990 data.

Notes: The so id vertical line represents a payout rate of 5% (the payout rate required of private foundations). This information is based on a sample of sponsoring organizations, weighted to reflect the full population of DAF sponsors. The apparent large number of organizations with a payout of 31.3% is actually one observation with a high sample weight. This underscores the imitations of using the IRS SOI sample data for analysis of donor advised fund behavior.

The Treasury Report found that the average payout rate across DAF sponsoring organizations was 9.3% in 2006.[43] The Treasury Report also found substantial variation in payout rates across DAF sponsoring organizations. In 2006, payouts were 0.0% at the 25th percentile, 0.6% at the 50th percentile (the median), and 10.5% at the 75th percentile. While the Treasury did not report the share with no payout or with less than 5%, more than 25% had no payout and more than 50% had a payout rate of less than 5%. Whether these measures differ from the 2008 estimates due to actual changes or sampling error is unclear, although the decline in asset values in 2008 might have increased the average payout rate.

The National Philanthropic Trust (NPT) also provides dollar weighted payout rates as part of its annual Donor Advised Fund Report. Payout ratios were 16.5% in 2007, rising to 17.6% in 2008, 18.6% in 2009, and falling to 17.1% in 2010.[44] Their payout rate of 17.6% for 2008 was somewhat lower than the estimates from the 990 sample. The Treasury Report's estimates were very close to the NPT's as calculated from the basic data in the 2011 NPT report, but the Treasury made adjustments for over-reporting. If the 2008 sample also had over reporting, the 19.2% share

---

[43] Treasury Report, p. 56.

[44] National Philanthropic Trust 2011 Report. We were unable to replicate their payout rates from the basic data in the earlier 2010 reports, but based on their reported assets and grants, the rate was 15.7% in 2006.

from the 2008 file, as well as the average rate of 13% could be too high and the share with low payout ratios too low. The trend of rising payout ratios as seen from 2007 through 2009 in the NPT data appeared to reflect the fall in assets and contributions, probably due to the financial crisis.

Organizations with low payout rates tend to be those that maintain a small number of individual accounts. For organizations that reported to have maintained one DAF account in 2008, the average mean payout was 10.6%. More than half (53%) of DAF sponsoring organizations that maintained a single account did not report having paid out any grants in 2008 (see **Figure 2**) and over 70% paid less than 5% (see **Figure 2**). If individual DAF account payout rates mirror payout rates as reported by sponsoring organizations that maintain a single account, it is likely that a large share individual DAF accounts do not pay out grants in any given year and that most of them pay less than 5%.

Figure 2. Payout Rate for Sponsoring Organizations Maintaining One DAF Account
2008

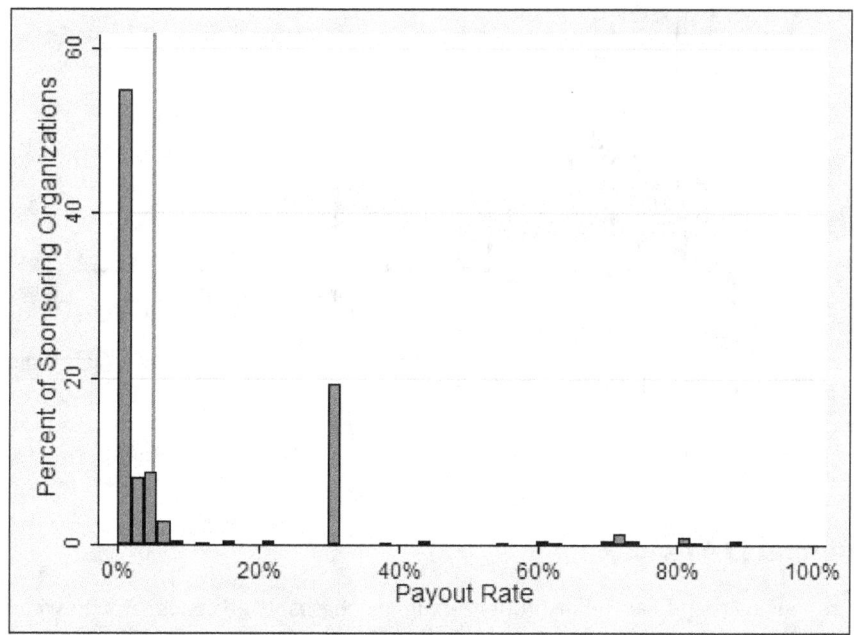

Source: CRS analysis of 2008 IRS SOI Form 990 data.

Notes: The so id vertical line represents a payout rate of 5% (the payout rate required of private foundations). This information is based on a sample of sponsoring organizations, weighted to reflect the full population of DAF sponsors. The apparent large number of organizations with a payout of 31.3% is actually one observation with a high sample weight. This underscores the imitations of using the IRS SOI sample data for analysis of donor advised fund behavior.

Most DAF accounts are maintained by organizations with a large number of DAF accounts. As illustrated in **Table 2**, nearly 87% of all DAF accounts are held by organizations that maintain at least 100 individual accounts. The average payout rate for sponsoring organizations with at least 100 individual accounts is 16.1%. Amongst sponsoring organizations that maintain at least 100 individual accounts, 3.6% have a payout rate of less than 5% (see **Figure 3**).[45] While the payout rates at the sponsoring organization level tend to exceed 5%, data on payouts from individual DAF accounts maintained within these organizations is not available.

Figure 3. Payout Rate for Sponsoring Organizations Maintaining One Hundred or More DAF Accounts

2008

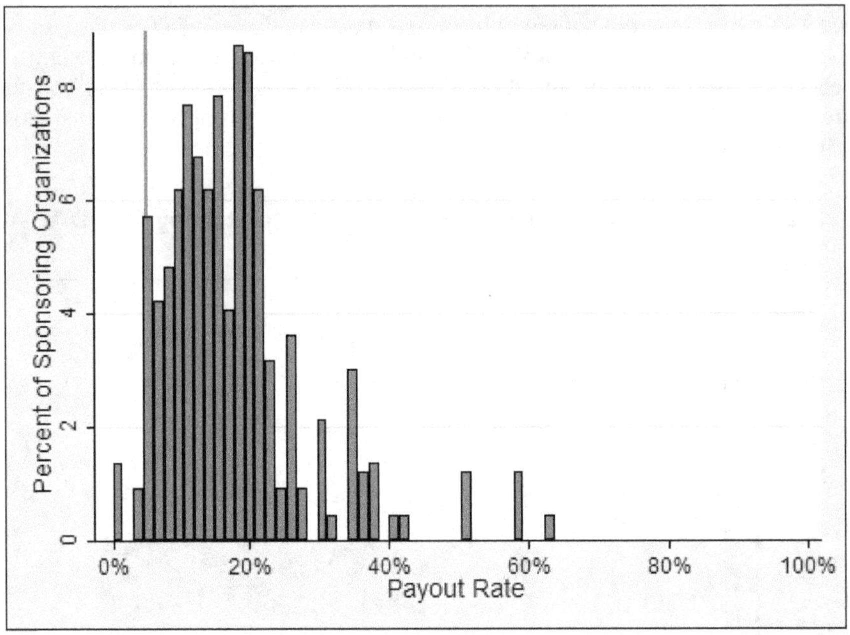

Source: CRS analysis of 2008 IRS SOI Form 990 data.

Notes: The so id vertical line represents a payout rate of 5% (the payout rate required of private foundations). This information is based on a sample of sponsoring organizations, weighted to reflect the full population of DAF sponsors.

Commercial DAFs

A number of commercial financial institutions maintain charitable affiliates through which they maintain individual DAF accounts on behalf of clients. In this study, a total of 21 organizations in the sample, representing 33 DAF sponsoring organizations in the population, that maintained individual DAF accounts on behalf of clients were identified. Statistics related to these organizations are analyzed separately from the entire DAF sponsoring organization population below because these organizations have been a specific focus of concern. These organizations may include some non-commercial national DAFs.

---

[45] Eight sampled organizations reported a payout rate of less than 5% in 2008. Each of these observations had a sampling weight of 1. Thus, it is estimated that eight out of the 222 DAF sponsoring organizations that maintain at least 100 individual accounts paid out less than 5% in 2008.

In 2008, 46.7% of individual DAF accounts were held in commercial DAFs (see **Table 5**). Thus, a very few DAF sponsoring organizations are responsible for a relatively large share of DAF accounts, as well as DAF assets, contributions, and grants.[46] In 2008, 34.3% of DAF assets, 39.2% of DAF contributions, and 39.7% of DAF grants were from sponsoring organizations identified as being commercial DAFs (see **Table 5**).

Table 5. Comparing All DAF Sponsoring Organizations to Commercial DAFs

2008

	All DAF Sponsoring Organizations	Commercial DAF Sponsoring Organizations	Share in Commercial DAFs
Number of DAFs Held	181,429	84,665	46.7%
DAF Assets	29,456.7	10,112.6	34.3%
DAF Contributions	7,094.3	2,783.5	39.2%
DAF Grants	7,101.5	2,781.6	39.7%

Source: CRS analysis of 2008 IRS SOI Form 990 data.

Notes: Dollar values in millions. For additional data and summary statistics, see **Appendix B**. Thirty-one out of 1,828 DAF sponsoring organizations were commercial DAFs.

The average payout rate for commercial DAFs was 26.5% in 2008. There is less variation in average payout rates across sponsoring organizations that are commercial DAFs, as compared to all DAF sponsoring organizations (see **Figure 4** for an illustration of this distribution). Since commercial DAFs tend to sponsor a large number of individual accounts (2,720 on average), it is possible that there is substantial variation in payout rates across individual accounts that is masked by the aggregate nature of available payout data. For commercial DAFs, the 25th percentile of the payout rate is 17.7%, and the 75th percentile 38.8% (see **Table B-1**). This compares to an average payout rate of 13.1% across all DAF sponsoring organizations. The 25th percentile and 75th percentile payout rates across all DAF sponsoring organizations were 0.0% and 19.5%, respectively, in 2008.

Using 2006 data, the 2011 Treasury Report found that commercial DAFs had a payout rate of 14.2%, while other DAFs with a national reach not affiliated with a financial institution had a payout rate of 28.7%.[47] This was higher than the overall payout rate found in 2006, of 9.3%. Similar to the 2008 results, there was less variation in the payout rates among commercial and national DAFs than across all DAF sponsoring organizations.

---

[46] Thirty-one out of 1,828 DAF sponsoring organizations were commercial DAFs.

[47] Treasury Report, p. 56.

Figure 4. Payout Rate for Commercial DAFs

2008

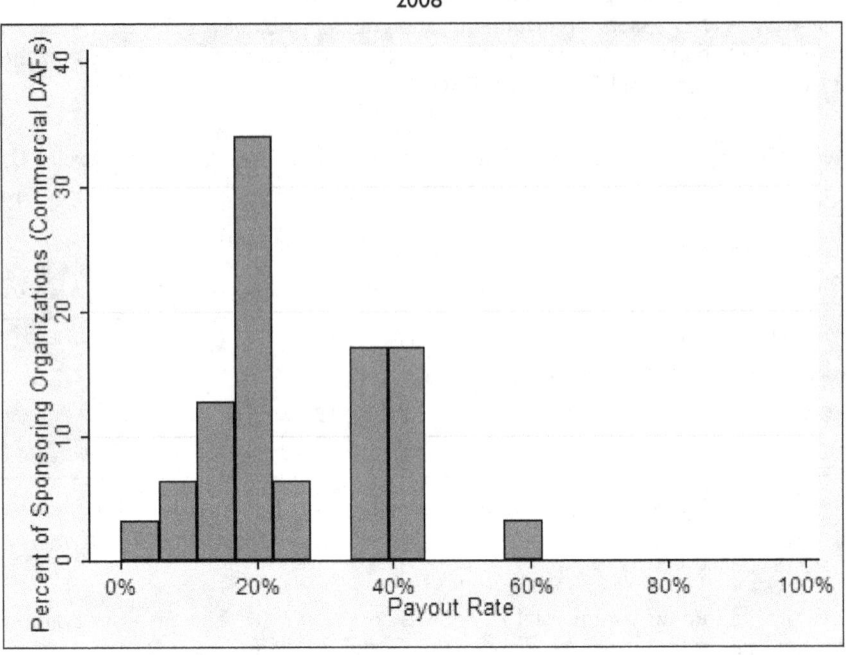

Source: CRS analysis of 2008 IRS SOI Form 990 data.

Notes: This information is based on a sample of sponsoring organizations, weighted to reflect the full population of DAF sponsors.

Policy Considerations

Perhaps the most important policy issues are those initially posed by Congress to the Treasury Department, including whether minimum distribution requirements should be imposed, whether rules restricting charitable contributions that apply to foundations should be imposed on DAFs, and whether contributions made to DAFs should be treated as completed gifts. In addition, a number of proposals were made in invited comments, including stricter treatment of commercial DAFs or national DAFs, limits on the duration of advisory rights or the lifetime of the DAF, prohibitions on retention of options or other rights, delays in deducting appreciated property until that property is sold, and limits on management fees. In addition, policies relating to additional reporting might be considered.

Minimum Distribution Requirements

The Treasury Report's position on minimum distribution requirements was that it was premature to make a recommendation based on only one year of data. The analysis of 2008 data presented in this report, however, shows results that are generally similar to those found by Treasury in their analysis of the 2006 data. In sum, both 2006 and 2008 data indicate a payout ratio in the aggregate that was higher than that of foundations, but a great deal of variability in payout ratios across sponsoring organizations. Further, a substantial fraction of sponsoring organizations made no payouts or payouts less than the foundation minimum of 5% in both 2006 and 2008. The

13.1% overall payout ratio found in the 2008 data was somewhat higher than the 9.3% rate Treasury found. This higher rate might reflect some overstatement of payouts in the data, as Treasury found for the 2006 sample, or it may have reflected the decline in asset values in 2008. Dollar weighted payout ratios prepared by the National Philanthropic Trust show a slight rise in payout rates in the years after 2006, but a decline between 2009 and 2010.

The Treasury Report stated that "Compared to private foundations, the mean payout rates for Aggregate DAFs in tax year 2006 appear to be high for most categories of DAF sponsoring organizations."[48] This statement seems to imply that observing an overall payout rate higher than that for foundations is a rationale for not imposing a minimum payout requirement. However, as noted earlier, there is ample reason to reject the notion that an aggregate payout ratio higher than that of private foundations provides a good rationale for not imposing such requirements on a per account basis. This point is clearly illustrated by the distribution of DAF sponsoring organizations with only one sponsor. For sponsoring organizations maintaining a single DAF account, the average payout rate was 10.6% (twice that required of private foundations). However, amongst sponsoring organizations that maintained a single DAF account, over half made no distribution and over 70% made a distribution of less than 5%.

Can characteristics of sponsoring organizations with only one DAF be generalized to larger DAF sponsoring organizations maintaining multiple accounts? Larger DAF sponsoring organizations tend to have somewhat higher aggregate payout rates (the payout rate in 2008 for sponsoring organizations with only one account was 10.6% in 2008, compared to 16.0% for organizations with 100 or more individual accounts). However, the different objectives of DAF accounts (year to year tax planning versus accumulating assets in the nature of a private foundation) that likely gave rise to the differential payout rates amongst DAF sponsoring organizations maintaining a single account also occur within sponsoring organizations with multiple accounts. Thus, there is likely to be substantial variation in payout rates at the individual account level across all sponsoring organizations.

Some additional aspects about payout ratios arise from the data analysis. Some of the public comments indicated that a 5% payout requirement would be acceptable if imposed on the overall sponsor rather than the individual account. The analysis of the 2008 data indicates that a minimum payout imposed on a per sponsor basis would be relatively meaningless. Out of the DAF sponsors with 100 or more accounts, covering 87% of accounts, only 3.6% fell below a 5% pay out rate. This approach would leave the vast majority of DAF accounts with no effective restrictions, while imposing requirements on the relatively few in DAF sponsors with a small number of DAFs. It would also create an incentive for donors who wished to accumulate funds and maintain endowments while paying little or nothing in grants to move to the larger DAF sponsors, including commercial DAFs.

Finally, although sponsors claimed that ensuring payout rates of their DAF accounts would be costly, their own comments indicated that they monitored their accounts for inactivity in many cases. The most straightforward approach would be to shift DAF account funds into a general fund that immediately made charitable distributions for accounts that did not meet the minimum requirements as the year end approaches. This approach is, as noted above, already used by the community foundation whose website was quoted above, although measures were only taken after long periods of inactivity.

---

[48] Treasury Report, p. 7.

Note also that a variation would be to impose the minimum distribution over a period of time, for example, equivalent to an annual percentage distribution over the past five years. This approach would allow some accumulation if desired to make a large gift, or to adjust for economic cycles (for example, smaller payouts when the economy is performing at full employment and larger ones during downturns when needs may be greater).

As noted below, some comments suggested applying minimum distributions only to commercial DAF sponsors or national DAFs in general, applying higher distribution requirements to them, or exempting traditional DAF sponsors (such as community foundations) from distribution requirements.

Some comments suggested that a minimum distribution amount might be perceived as a guideline and would lower overall distributions, given that private foundations tend to grant around 5%. However, since some DAF individual account objectives include short term charitable giving management, a comparison with private foundations may be inappropriate.

Imposing Tighter Rules that Apply to Foundations on DAFs

The Treasury Report rejected stricter rules that apply to foundations for DAFs on the grounds that the legal control of the fund is in the hands of the sponsoring organizations, a public charity. Donors do not legally control contributions from these accounts or the investment. These benefits include the ability to donate larger shares of income in cash gifts and gifts of appreciated property, the ability to deduct the fair market value of non-traded appreciated assets, and exemption from excise taxes on investment income.

As discussed previously, donors appear to have actual control of grant making because sponsoring organizations typically follow their advice, as indicated in web sites of sponsoring organizations and reinforced by the commentary received and reported in the Treasury Report. In many cases they effectively have investment control as well. In that sense, donors, who are presumably concerned about the use of their own accounts and not about the sponsoring organization, have the same control, in effect, of the most important aspect, the recipient of charitable gifts. In considering this issue, one question is whether the restricted legal rights of the donor or actual practice should determine the appropriate treatment.

Completed Gifts

Although the Treasury Report also concluded that donations to DAF accounts were completed gifts, just as a gift to a foundation is, commentators questioned whether the gift was complete if there were options (options to buy or sell the gifted property at a future date) related to the use of gifts of property.

Some comments suggested that puts or calls, or other option retentions with respect to property be explicitly disallowed. Suggestions were also made that deductions for a gift of appreciated property not be allowed until the property is sold.

Tighter Restrictions on Commercial DAFs or National DAFs

Comments expressing concern about the lack of a charitable purpose for commercial DAFs or even for national DAFs, as compared to community foundations, and DAF sponsors with religious, educational, and other charitable purposes led to some suggestions for tighter regulations and greater restrictions for these DAF sponsors. Some noted a tension, especially with the commercial DAF, between the needs of charitable organizations to restrict contributions and the incentive to maintain large investment accounts.[49] These proposals could include only applying minimum distributions requirements to these DAFs, applying higher distribution requirement, or exempting traditional sponsors.

Limit the Duration of Advisor Rights, Or Limit the Life of a DAF Account

Some comments proposed that the duration of DAF accounts be restricted either by limiting the period of years advisory rights would be effective, or limiting the life of a DAF account (for example, by not allowing future generations to inherit the advisory role). Presumably if such limits were imposed the DAF sponsor would be required to pay out the entire amount in the account over a specified period. This approach would be an alternative or perhaps addition to a payout requirement to insure that the amounts in DAF accounts are used for charitable purposes in some reasonable time period.

Objections to these restrictions might come from donors who wish to establish the tradition of philanthropy in their families; some donors purposefully include their children as advisors.

Limits on Maintenance Fees

Some comments also suggested that limits be imposed on charges related to DAF account maintenance and investments. Program expenses for some DAF sponsors were high but may have included direct charitable activities. In general, relatively little is known about the costs of maintaining and investing DAF funds.

Improvements in Reporting

One obvious constraint in analyzing issues associated with DAFs is that all reporting is done at the aggregate DAF sponsor level, which means there is information only by inference concerning the shares of accounts that have low or no payout ratios. Requiring reporting on individual DAF accounts is an option that could improve understanding of how DAFs operate and provide better oversight.

Consolidated reporting may mean there are fewer organizations for the IRS to monitor and fewer forms to process. Others disagreed. To quote the Treasury Report: "One claimed that under current law, DAFs are 'virtually invisible to tax authorities and nonprofit regulators' and expressed concern that the PPA had done nothing to alleviate this 'problem.' Another respondent

---

[49] See Treasury Report, p. 77.

described DAFs as 'a world of hidden philanthropy that merits significantly updated disclosure' and stressed that 'without individual level reporting, there will be no adequate way for the IRS to determine' if a charitable purpose is being pursued and if the DAFs' managers are complying with the law."[50]

Several pieces of information would be helpful in providing a better understanding of DAF payout information. Useful information that could be provided by DAF sponsors could include the share of their DAF accounts that made no distributions, the share that made distributions of less than 5%, or a general distribution of accounts across different payout intervals. Information on investment fees and administrative costs of managing the DAFs, separated from other costs, could also be useful. Additional information could help policymakers evaluate whether giving through DAFs is achieving charitable giving policy goals.

Conclusion

In some ways, the fundamental policy issue about how freely to allow donors to make contributions that are not immediately used for charitable purposes is whether such arrangements increase charitable giving per dollar of cost or decrease it.[51] Allowing for contributions to accumulate and earn a tax free return increases the benefit to the donor and thus may increase contributions to funds or foundations, albeit at an additional cost. Such arrangements can also reduce current charitable giving by encouraging fund accumulation, a concern that presumably motivated the minimum distribution rules for private foundations. DAFs differ from foundations in some ways, including the legal technicalities, but in practice, are very similar. One concern that remains for both foundations and DAFs is how soon donations are put to charitable use.

---

[50] Treasury Report, pp. 67-68.

[51] Such issues were addressed in the 2005 hearing, Charities and Charitable Giving: Proposals for Reform, Senate Finance Committee, April 2005. See testimony by Jane G. Gravelle, Congressional Research Service, http://finance.senate.gov/imo/media/doc/jgtest040505.pdf for discussions on donor-advised funds.

Appendix A. Description of Data

The data used in this report come from the 2008 Internal Revenue Service (IRS) Statistics of Income (SOI) Form 990 public use file.[52] The IRS SOI exempt organization file contains information on 501(c)(3) through (c)(9) organizations that filed the Form 990 informational return.[53] The dataset is based on a stratified random sample. For larger organizations, the sampling rate is 100%. Thus, all large tax-exempt organizations filing the Form 990 are included in the sample. Sampling weights are used to adjust for sampling rates of smaller organizations.

Tax-exempt organizations are asked on the 2008 Form 990 informational return if they maintained any donor advised funds (DAFs).[54] If an organization indicates that DAFs were maintained, they are advised to complete Schedule D, Part 1 (see **Figure A-1**). On Schedule D, DAF sponsoring organizations are asked to provide information on the total number of DAFs held, contributions to and grants from DAFs during the year, and the aggregate value of DAF assets at the end of the year.

Figure A-1. Form 990 Schedule D: Donor Advised Fund Questions

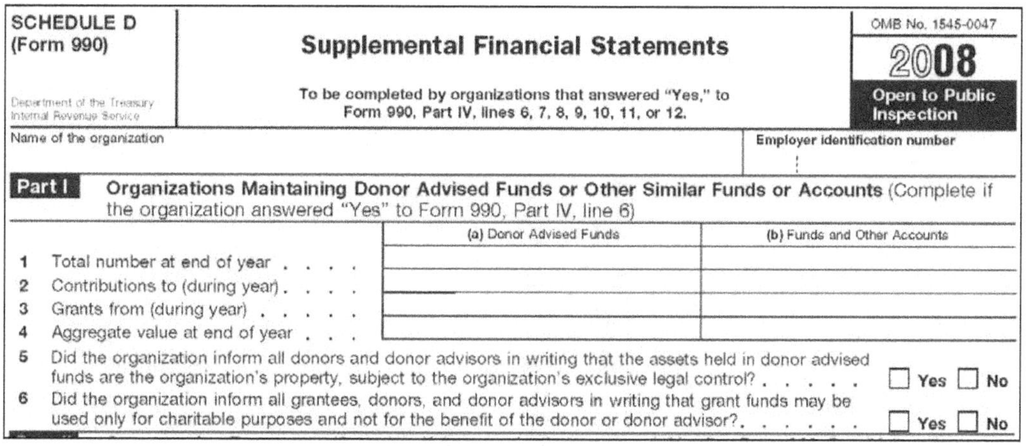

SCHEDULE D (Form 990)

Department of the Treasury Internal Revenue Service

Supplemental Financial Statements

To be completed by organizations that answered "Yes," to Form 990, Part IV, lines 6, 7, 8, 9, 10, 11, or 12.

OMB No. 1545-0047

2008

Open to Public Inspection

Name of the organization

Employer identification number

Part I **Organizations Maintaining Donor Advised Funds or Other Similar Funds or Accounts** (Complete if the organization answered "Yes" to Form 990, Part IV, line 6)

		(a) Donor Advised Funds	(b) Funds and Other Accounts
1	Total number at end of year		
2	Contributions to (during year)		
3	Grants from (during year)		
4	Aggregate value at end of year		

5 Did the organization inform all donors and donor advisors in writing that the assets held in donor advised funds are the organization's property, subject to the organization's exclusive legal control? . . . . . ☐ Yes ☐ No

6 Did the organization inform all grantees, donors, and donor advisors in writing that grant funds may be used only for charitable purposes and not for the benefit of the donor or donor advisor? . . . . . . ☐ Yes ☐ No

Source: IRS Form 990, Schedule D.

In the 2008 IRS SOI Form 990 public use file, 599 sampled organizations either 1) answered "yes" to the questions asking if the organization maintained any DAFs, or 2) reported that at least one DAF was held on Schedule D. This sample of 599 organizations represents a population of 2,158 DAF sponsoring organization.

Before further evaluating the data, the data were further cleaned to eliminate observations with clear reporting errors. Five observations were dropped for having reported nonsensical values for

[52] This data and data documentation is available through the IRS SOI website: http://www.irs.gov/taxstats/charitablestats/article/0,,id=97176,00.html.

[53] There is a separate data file for organizations that file the Form 990EZ. Since organizations maintaining DAFs are required to file the Form 990, and cannot file the Form 990EZ, data on organizations filing the Form 990EZ was not included in the analysis.

[54] See question #6, in part 4, the Checklist of Required Schedules, of the 2008 Form 990. Available at http://www.irs.gov/pub/irs-prior/f990—2008.pdf.

the total number of DAFs held. Another fifty-one observations were dropped that indicated DAFs were maintained, but then reported having zero DAFs and zero DAF assets at the end of the year. Another two observations were dropped that reportedly maintained DAF accounts, but did not report any DAF contributions, grants, or DAF assets.

After dropping observations with clear reporting errors, the sample contained 541 observations representing a population of 1,828 DAF sponsoring organizations. Other adjustments were made to collect for clear reporting errors.[55] The resulting sample is the basis for the summary statistics presented in this report. Summary statistics are presented in **Appendix B**.

A separate examination of commercial DAFs is also provided. A total of 21 commercial funds were identified in the sample. (Some of these may be national DAFs that are not commercial.) Several of these funds had a weight that was greater than one. Thus, these 21 observations represent a total population of 31 sponsoring organizations.[56] Summary statistics for commercial DAFs, based on the information as reported on the 2008 IRS Form 990s of these 21 organizations, are reported in **Appendix B**.

---

[55] For example, in 2008, one of the largest commercial DAFs, Fidelity Investment Charitable Gift Fund, reported that they only maintained one DAF account. On their 2007 and 2009 Form 990s, Fidelity Investment Charitable Gift fund reported to have maintained 47,918 and 52,466 DAF accounts, respectively. To correct for this reporting error, we assumed that Fidelity Investment Charitable Gift Fund maintained 50,182 DAFs in 2008.

[56] The 21 organizations in the sample identified as maintaining DAF accounts on behalf of their clients were: The American Endowment Fund; T. Rowe Price Program for Charitable Giving, Inc.; The U.S. Charitable Gift Trust; Goldman Sachs Philanthropy Fund; Renaissance Charitable Foundation, Inc.; Oppenheimer Funds Legacy Program; Donors Capital Fund, Inc.; Vanguard Charitable Endowment Program; LM Charitable Gift Trust; Ayco Charitable Foundation; Morgan Stanley Smith Barney Global IM; Fidelity Investments Charitable Gift Fund; FJC Foundation of Philanthropic Gifts; Schwab Charitable Fund; Goldman Sachs Charitable Gift Fund; Harris MyCFO Foundation; East Bay Community Foundation; National Philanthropic Trust; Raymond James Charitable Endowment Fund; RSF Global Community Fund, Inc.; and Ernst & Young Foundation.

Appendix B. Data Summary Statistics

Summary statistics for information on DAFs reported on 2008 IRS Form 990s are provided in **Table B-1**. A description of the data can be found in **Appendix A**. Further discussion and interpretation of these summary statistics is provided in the main body of this report.

Table B-1. DAF Data as Reported on Form 990: Summary Statistics

2008

Variable	All DAF Sponsoring Organizations	Commercial DAF Sponsoring Organizations
Number of DAFs Held		
Mean	99	2,720
Median	5	358
25th Percentile	1	49
75th Percentile	32	1,439
Total	181,429	84,665
# of Observations	1,828	31
DAF Assets		
Mean	$16,114,172	$321,647,168
Median	$432,585	$61,512,653
25th Percentile	$47,685	$10,186,159
75th Percentile	$3,266,999	$202,316,978
Total	$29,456,705,536	$10,112,586,752
# of Observations	1,828	31
Average Assets per DAF		
Mean	$369,455	$426,724
Median	$55,178	$154,849
25th Percentile	$20,789	$95,738
75th Percentile	$184,929	$902,231
Total	—	—
# of Observations	1,818[a]	31
DAF Contributions		
Mean	$3,880,602	$88,532,666
Median	$29,898	$12,851,414
25th Percentile	$0	$2,432,869
75th Percentile	$711,340	$41,649,571
Total	$7,094,332,176	$2,783,467,008
# of Observations	1,828	31

Variable	All DAF Sponsoring Organizations	Commercial DAF Sponsoring Organizations
DAF Grants		
Mean	$3,973,658	$78,931,932
Median	$25,000	$9,999,612
25th Percentile	$0	$4,150,126
75th Percentile	$421,614	$40,583,487
Total	$7,010,526,208	$2,781,619,968
# of Observations	1,828	31
Payout Rate (%)		
Mean	13.1%	26.5%
Median	6.1%	22.0%
25th Percentile	0.0%	17.7%
75th Percentile	19.5%	38.8%
Total	—	—
# of Observations	1,738b	31

Source: CRS analysis of 2008 IRS SOI Form 990 Data.

Notes: Figures are based on a sample of 2008 Form 990s weighted to reflect estimated population totals.

a. Organizations that reported maintaining DAFs, but then reported "0" as the number of DAFs held, are excluded, reducing the number of observations.

b. In computing this payout rate, only DAF sponsoring organizations that reported maintaining at least one DAF and organizations that reported positive asset values for 2008 were included. Four observations representing 10 organizations were excluded when the sample was restricted to organizations that reportedly held at least one DAF. An additional six observations, representing 79 organizations, were excluded for having zero reported DAF assets.

Author Contact Information

Molly F. Sherlock
Specialist in Public Finance
msherlock@crs.loc.gov, 7-7797

Jane G. Gravelle
Senior Specialist in Economic Policy
jgravelle@crs.loc.gov, 7-7829